PLAY FOR TIME

PLAY FOR TIME
Poems

PAULA MENDOZA

Published by Gaudy Boy LLC,
an imprint of Singapore Unbound
www.singaporeunbound.org/gaudyboy
New York

For more information on ordering books, contact jkoh@singaporeunbound.org.

ISBN 978-0-9828142-7-7

Cover design by Flora Chan
Interior design by Jennifer Houle
Proofread by Cindy Hochman of "100 Proof" Copyediting Services

For Isabel and Rey and Peter and Paul

CONTENTS

Then

Beginning

Middle

PLAY FOR TIME

FIRST

SPELL

after antarctica and before the viscose :: in between heart's atria and chamber music :: a paltry offering when you took what you could get :: forces unseen rhubarbed the crenellations :: the note read ship her back to mother :: when i am not around bad things happen :: a hero like captain planet's mullet :: i am taking the pie with me :: i unsubtle it :: some mornings abacus and other nights veruschka in the bed on fire :: tinder even if shivered leafless :: forsythia for instance :: in my net are pneuma i pin onto tiny sateen pillows :: iridesce your dead :: commandment after commandment trembles my little chisel :: shattered the slab :: i can be forgetting the low-hanging misticles :: salamandrine or begotten :: i shimmy onto my hind hooves come time to be stood :: end to end and into eating my tail :: haberdasher her kremlin siam :: chortle your knockwurst and slut it for the creamdom :: helsinki gone down singing megadeth :: mourners hum accompaniment :: mostly free jazz and coke jingles :: teach it to sing and feed it full of murrka :: man's business is mastery.

Engineer

I took it apart.

When it was whole,
it wasn't right.

Gaps everywhere, nothing
locked into place.

I laid out each piece
on the floor
in order of how they felt
in my hand—

their weight, roughness,
and what I imagined they did
when once they held together.

This

must have grinded all the rest
forward, I think,

as I set a gear down,
third in line.

I don't know what to do
with any of them.

It is morning and still cold
when I walk outside
with what, inside my fist,

feels smoothest, heaviest—

and knock something living
out of a tree.

It made a sound,
softer than I would have
figured a small, furred body

falling into dirt might make.

Whole, it wasn't right.

Apart, lined up against each other,
they were near enough good.

I left the body
to be eaten by the stray we named.

Inside lay more pieces
to find.

For each, some better use.

Behind the Shelf

The tall man fills receptacles with substances that resemble you, that is, substances *of* you, and you grow certain that they *are* you: carved atria, swatches of thigh, hinges of knuckle and elbow and knee. There are vials of every convolution, sops of greymeat, each pit and furrow of memory. And blood. Mostly there's blood. Your blood is catalogued by the breath which shimmered or seethed, by what press of flesh effervesced these shining viscosities, all who thickened or thinned that crimson, as in, this specimen is the first time you fell in love. This, when you hated your mother. Here, held an infant. Here, tried to kill yourself. There are many containers. The taxonomy does not arouse terror, you are not afraid for the pulp of you to be archived or articulated this way. Still, an arctic terror rises and sours in back of a throat. The terror derives from the tall man. The tall man is not god but he is a conjecture made up of god. He is a radiant speculation accumulated from god-like detritus. He is nothing, like a god. *I am afraid,* you call out. Glass swallows every syllable. You call out. Your tongue, a fat slug, glints in the dirtiest jar on the farthest shelf, and your eyes, in the cleanest, look on.

Dehelixing Adora: At the Tip of His Tongue

He invents the snow for word, and folds his hands.
I crossed my poles from dusk to east, and fasted
in the winter of his cell. There, my body became
uninhabitable. Nevertheless, men

burrow a certain death and call it home.
He is certain, tasking the rook with flight.
I pry my jaw's vise, emancipating all wingless beasts.
We sew scripts of exile into the lining of robes.

He invents the night for word as I lick the salt
behind his knees. For those weak of limb must crawl
to know dawn's mauve approach. Forgiveness
invents a hasp for hearts. And, nevertheless, my vices.

When opening a fist, finger by finger, found a tooth.
Which is not the word for gone, though they may sound alike.

LEFT BY THE SHIP

The dull hunger of leaving
home makes of any distance

an ache. Where weather is
mostly monsoon pours a poverty

so lush, even the garbage flowers.
I wished once to be absolved

a mother, to hover above
like a scale of oil or Christ.

◆

The cinematography was excellent, sumptuous and moody, with its
palette of earthy greys and jewel greens. One girl, Margarita De La
Rosa, second-generation Amerasian, had such intensity that storm
clouds seemed to collect in her gaze. The director chose his subjects
well. Any sympathetic aesthete, moved by how gorgeous the
surrounding ruin, would not be able to resist investing in the children
and their common trouble. Such mud, such mosses. Set in relief by
bleakest tones, the deteriorated, brighter, shone. I translate reading
beneath the scene. I scan their sounds and think of water striders, how
meaning repels, and the way pebbles and insects skim a faint miracle
between water and air.

◆

6

Uninflected, assuming
whosever reigning tongue

tastes like anywhere
I am. I can swirl or
hold that honey'n
draw 'er out real—rill—
rule—slow. In Texas, it's *orl*.
And mesquite's growed in *sorl*.

Ah lack what I lack.
I lack it when you small.

◆

Meanwhile—the sun and its blades and motes floated geometries—
that brutish summer—I kept all doors open and—a hornet flew into
my apartment. I spoke to it, as if it could hear and only refused to
listen. As if it understood and could be coaxed or bullied back outside.
I threatened it. I derided it for its stupidity as it hit the glass in soft
thuds. And it sounded like the pad of a finger tapping against a window
to catch someone's attention outside. It wanted to be outside but
couldn't find its way to the open door. It droned beyond where I could
see, and later—silence. It may still be in here. It may have rested on the
low sill. If I see it, I will have to kill it.

◆

occident, does she golden   *flute of throat*   sacrum hives
under, some supple umber?   *fleet of thought*   a fire snarl

         always they are wanting to eat me

                             I want you in my mouth
      go ahead

                             I want to bite
      go ahead

◆

My mother was an island girl.
My father was a city boy.

They ran away, they ran away.
And I did, too.

And we never went back.
And we never went back.
And we never went back.

My Demon Is Sad All It Can Be Is Complicit

If reading between parallel realities, your mother. Somebody will always be saying goodbye. They are being sucked into the distance or you are being pulled away. Here is what I know: I've shot this scene before. My feet blistered to get here. Not rut or habit but mandala. I ripple out and out { { petalpetalpetalpetalpetalpetalpetalpetal } } such a showy peony! Boatload is a family and I am too sensitive meaning my feelings are not activist. Go straight to the rot of your happiness. The ground conveys bodies apart. It will be many knots before the wailing subsumes. We are each of us abandoned. All I know folds the page corner of the glyph shift's falter towards intelligible. I swear I made it happen inside. My Siamesis no longer spoken. We are severed. They've hunted Babylons to extinction. Our mothers diversify their brood. Koan is the head split, not the egg hatched. In certain light our features cannot be believed. Healed like no venom's business. Hallucine, nauseaesque. Cortisol irksome. Fever gullies magma into desertscape, some vast beige. Fire, then, is mine. Mine is thy fire. Then bested under mantle's shellac. Crushed a harder heat, weh? Psalter grommet this clin-clin, weh? Nihil inkarra ashwa patay. Bata, umuwi kana. Tumahimik kana. Indoors I'm the nine of bulls. Batten down the crystal, Mobius, I'm goring for the kill.

Lucy

Make it snakes. Whom were always deceiver and forfeit.
As I am always derivative. A sap. The sticky. Stain
of his leak. What's crusted the slip. What makes it so
hard/beat fast/feel sad. If a matter of origin, I'll throw up
a cosmos. Twinkle-lights pock my smile with zodiac.
Make it the first time I let him, his O-face smeared
into an Edvard taffy theatre mask. His joy was terrible.
Its in-and-in-and-in, whorls of wet, agitated sand
that could not bear my weight. Make it a heavy sound.
Make it roach scuttle in cathedrals. Make it rainstick's
thirsty lie, faux firelight, and the gas turned up. Make it
black-out sex forgetting she had a name. I get ahead
running towards a dangling carrot's veiny slow dissolve.
I move my lips but only his sounds come out. I motor
hind hooves and the cyclone dust kicked up vanishes me.
About my head, a red halo dilates. She is not my own
god, I am my own. My god, make it snakes. Make one so
onyx a glossing, so diamond a tip, my every shiver's incision.

LUCY, AGAIN

Shall I be minded elsely? The femme-dom poem's
what I forget how to write. A loss of thrust. A sabre's long
tooth for stiletto. I walk on reflections the asphalt glimmers
on soaked evenings. Do I grow venerable? Check my organs.
O, plight of Philomels clawing out of my disgusting mouth!
Each one pulped to a hi-shine ooze I paint my nails with.
So crone and cyclic the depictions of his thin-fingered
hold on what's left of my love. Which elsewise is
cleaner language than my fangy and mealmouthed.
For no other does my murder lascivious. None other can
ill this trickle like his hot blue volt. In ink such ardors
curdle. This one's for my girls, my unwrittens and their knees.
Their shoulders round a suicide slope and their longings
are truisms, ism-ing all over the carpet. My whip hangs flaccid
in the broom closet. Jars of preserves. Balsam and ambers.
Sunrises alarm the cocks whose necks my wrist snaps.
Because these daughters of mine, risen from the dead white
myth, expect dinner on the table. And meat is meat is meat.

Leave the Sky to Who Shall Wear

that vast blue drag.

In shade, I paled
frightened through aisles of cypress.

Sung in the dark, the paths
vein. So long unseen, in

the long unlit I unearthed her.
She was full of doors

and tender with hum.
Her heart

a clock engined with tripwire
and fish hooks.

Eyes, the colour puce.
You can be in love with this.

If she dies tomorrow, I will leave
my skin for her to crawl back into.

So

Scene Rewrite

Shot: a single red balloon curves through cloudless sky. The weather is spring in October: mild, forgone. A small fist uncurls and the ribbon rises past the frame. Cut red balloon, cut sky. Write the dog howls like a baby in an alley. Mournful thing. No, get rid of the dog. Write a body in a chair in knots, unknotting. Zoom in on sinew, an agony; i.e., when the skin draws taut. The body doing all it can not to kill itself slow or even please itself quick. Introduce the stranger and the bed the body does not sleep in. Cut lateral crawl of *I mean*. Insert crossfade. The body says: no one can make thinking a stone to hold then throw at a window. Cut the body in the chair, insert broken window. Shot: paper. A fine point's silver buds black. Blur of hand brushed against. Thatched cream, blot dilates into surface, the bleed beneath a stalled stroke. Voiceover: "The weather was forgivingly warm. If forgiveness comes, let it be in heat." No one writes letters these days. No one wrote in a letter asking—*Is the language doing it for you? Did you write yourself out of the bed you didn't sleep in?* Cut to balloon barking in an alley. Add the sky ripped with howl. Cut the baby. Dissolve to stock shots of a bloom's frame-by-frame rot. Run her in reverse. Pull back, cut to notepad: *resist analysis.* Tight shot, close on face, crumpled. Ink irised to a pin. Cut to body. Wind through petals, the mouth moving. Translation: *I can't tell.* The body rises from the chair. *Tell me again.* The chair the body throws at the stranger goes right through, breaks nothing.

STORYBOARD

A trick, to secret a woman
in a red suit entering a boutique
behind the action up front held
in deep focus saturated against her.
It can be an argument, even a brawl.
Perhaps a choker shot of the accused's
grimace, lips clamped over teeth
one nearly hears grinding.

One arc disappears the woman
in red behind a door above which
cursive neon flashes a word in French
that suggests the establishment sells
handbags or sex or pastries. Desire
tarnishes in blush. Perhaps one
would rather watch the writer turn
the projector off.

The woman is returned
in the final reveal. Until then, we
become in the dark so much slip
between his grit, slicked as much as
crushed. Each scene makes a coarse
meal of dread. Seeing erodes. A trick—
to leave out the part when he was inside.

Blurred at first, the woman
sharpens as she walks towards us
and we trust that inside her handbag
are the papers and poison. Neither
of which will save—before the list
of names scrolls past—anyone
you decided you loved.

Narrative Poem

I want to go back in time but not like inside a plot where the heroine is triggered by the sight of a blue coat and the killer's face draws out of shadow so everyone knows it was him all along. How her vision dissolves backwards, periphery narrowing its aperture to sketch in the folds, the gestures, the damning scene. There needn't be a body, no chambers emptied of shells, no curl of smoke or blood snaking under the door. No one ever has to leave and refuse to turn around while someone else stands in the rain and watches them walk away. I don't want to go back in time to cohere or arc elsewise. What I have in mind's *in mind*, like in that film where the lovers consent to the removal of all neural trace of their love, effectively rendering each other as never having happened. A future-perfect tense as preventive procedure. *I will not have known you.* So, not like entering into *then* with *now*'s dimension-crossing machine, where one navigates knots in the endless rope of time, all of which mistakes sequence for story. As if one ever had to do with the other. No, I mean—a cautery. A burning I can hold in hand and sear what's past, your face briefly aglow then dark, the nerve's path scarred over.

Sentimental Poem

That one Christmas we got each other a DVD of *Under the Skin* in which Scarlett Johansson is a serial killer alien harvesting the viscera of lonely men. It moved you. It terrified and depressed me. We were both moved is the thing. The day after we saw it in the theatre I wrote a mediocre poem about how the body you live in can be broken into. Days after, we watched another about a girl looking for a briefcase of money. Each scene steeped in grey and blue, every still was all the hues that meant cold, alone. You were comforted to see one kind of loneliness reflected back. Her hunt put me in a funk for weeks. I believed I was her and saw the poem was a fiction like money or murder. I went looking for it in inclement weather. If I'm being honest, romantic comedies are my jam. Calling things your jam is something the kids say these days. I note this for authenticity. Which isn't being honest but rather being true to the performance. A week after Christmas one of us returned the movie because we only needed the one copy. We were being practical, which is romantic. We were true to form like a joke that kills. Not two but one we would never need cut in half. The months ahead were underwater, grey and blue. A year or two ahead, there's the one copy you've kept, and we are still two, you over there, me over here. And again, cold around the bend. And cold buried the girl who embroidered a map marking red what I and you seek. And we are each our own moldering maps. Folds and illegible roads fused and flaking, accrual of so much in-between. There's the gift I will give you and you will give me that neither of us will need. There's a briefcase of cash or a gutter of innards or Scarlett Johansson naked, which both of us appreciate, having an eye for exquisite lines.

Making New Friends

I think of a joke and devise contexts to precipitate my telling this joke. I think of the person I will tell it to. I rehearse the telling, run a hand through hair, contort into good angles. Every day entire conversations play in my head that render the person superfluous. I make them a stage, a pool of light to cross into. The joke I think of is not a laugh-out-loud kind of joke. It's more the kind that will turn up the corners of your mouth in a wry half-smile. A wry half-smile is something I read in a novel once, or several times, when I used to read novels. It communicates a level of intimacy between two people but not one of any shared pain or struggle. Not even the sort arriving at the end of desire or some such conflict. It's like how people say simpatico or talk of energies and frequencies and really getting somebody. The expression suggests closeness without all that mess. Instantaneous, clean as spark. In a wrist's stroke across that rough pad, I trick you lit. I handle all variant afters. Any joke has taught me best to fold in ways that catch the light. Any telling tilts the head, arcs a spine. I know when to lower and slow—voice and limb—the better to turn up the corners of your mouth. To turn up anything. And when I draw up close I will your smile broken wide, bright, full-throated laugh I make, I made you and you are thinking now of taking off all my clothes.

Alternate Ending I

A little girl sticks pins into the plush
of a forearm, believes the woman
she will be must feel each prick
and, stabbing deeper than she thought
she could stand, gasped, looked up
and into the glass, I saw her catch
my breath, I looked her in the eye
and cooed, "Darling, stop that.
Come here. Let me hold you.
Let's calm ourselves down, shall we?"

Alternate Ending II

Another man's body moves
over another woman, the child
watches them kiss, it thinks
I must be someone
someone would want to kiss.
The window outside glows and dims
ten times to count ten years and it
crosses the street, it wears a dress,
red lipstick, and kohl, and she runs
towards a man who moves his body
around her and she grows very
small inside him as they kiss.

Alternate Ending III

The revolution has come.
The headline reads: Daughter Found Dead.
The story goes on to say how witnesses
found her hung by her own hair.
The tower was a basement.

Erratum: The tower was a well.

Erratum: She lived. She let down
her hair into the well. She let a man
climb up her hair, climb out
of the tower. Daughter says:
"He is my friend now.
He will never leave my side."

Dehelixing Adora: A Colonial Kantá

A battery of violents and still the heart
data proves inconclusive.

Do our deficients coerce? I malign
your sovereignty. Alas, my talon's

no match for your drone.
Police the alleys in this speech.

My theory stiffens your discipline.
Slavishly, this thought pulverizes love

into something I can breathe.
I can't breathe.

Maugre my dread, I convolute to you, sahib.
O, durable truth of my adoration!

Mistake me again, I am
ugly with lust.

This weeping is consensual.
Your episteme is my ontology.

I, island adjacent, of redoubtable
splendor. Dear pirate. Plunder.

Lyric

Perhaps this, too, is a move.
Listen: here's another.
Not unlike the way—
vines clamber, glossy, up a trellis.
That is, cloying.
I'm sorry. Maybe if I hold myself up
against this one beam of light
to burnish a collarbone soft
as how you used to kiss along
its slope—we can find our way
back there. I can be backlit by lens flare
for you. We can be swallowed gold
in the sepia of it, and my hair will be
something more than the clog
pooling murky water
around our ankles. It can find its shine
in a line—it will be a heavy curtain
of secrets. Or wilder, as in weather.
It has been storms before.
It has been various hours of night.
I have been wanting to write outside
of thinking, but it's hard out here
for a poet. I'm stupid with spring
and impatient with those
that refuse to burst, too stubborn
to purple such sudden luxury
out the ground. I know, I know—

always with the goddamn flowers.
But, really, what of our fresh foolishness
can compete with their dumb bloom?
We should all be that ready to die.

THEN

Halfway

You were between two animals.
Between two attributions.
At the crotch of a river's fork.
At a loss, at least.
Between all losses, tendering alms.
By the skin of one's stolen teeth.
The lethargy of one newly shorn.
To derive, say, attenuate, say
starved to a taper. A porousness.
False asphodel if aphasic, if sticky.
Vaseline-smear a focalization.
Ocean maw and mountain blade
recede. At last, at least—this. A figure
gathers line and edge. She is between
two roars. Who devours or drowns.
Say shore when you mean precipice.
Say split when you mean in pieces.
Redoubled at the jut of some far
becoming. Between, to say the least.
A shade and its absorption. To
swatch a sea's phonemes, to score
what of light she keeps to let through.

STOP ME IF YOU'VE HEARD

Everything I write is the end but I want something more than smog and a shitty poem about drowning in floodwater. When it gets under the skin like an implant you pick at screaming into your arm you can't have it and I won't let you. It isn't paranoia it's a scab and a swarm of hornets trembling the shape of a valentine heart. It's when I met you I knew it wasn't gum I'd stepped on. You can come inside my vortex but only if you clean up after. I briefly considered going girlfriend after a night pounded jelly-kneed fetal on the floor. They think they know, better each day, but I turn. Like milk. Like medieval breaking wheel. Like coat. Like knock. Like down. What's there to say but next. Who's left to kiss, to leave, or on first, or beside the building boarded up and tagged with scripture. There are two types of poet, it goes. And there's the mistake you think you're making new but it's the same name different hole. The same gore different axe. The same smoke different gun. *It really goes.* Off, faster than I got there, a pool of ripped cotton around my ankles. *Do you know? Where you're going to? Do you like the things that life is showing you?* Maybe if I were less of more of the same. Maybe if you were—onetwothreefourfive   sixseveneightnineten eeeeleven   twe-eh-eh-eh-eh-elve. Please god don't let me write another reason why I am afraid we fucked it all up and good. Please god I am so bad at dystopia like what is aftermath of decline even. Nothing adds up except neglect. No one really believes you when you say I meant it when I said _____.

The End

An arc is only:

Eventually somebody.
Inevitably something.

Told—in cards, crystal, the lines
cut and feathered on palms

or bled through paper. Kept
in begin is idling, is neither

dug deeper or getting up.
Too often, knees. Their buckle.

Less the thought than how
a word sidesteps the middle

and ends. Once upon a blue-
skied, sun-lit hell

I contrived a precipice, decided:
She is the story, full of holes.

Curator

If I put this photograph of the shriveled iris
next to this photograph of the crumpled metal of a car door
next to this torn page—

on which one had scribbled three attempts at beginning
a letter, the first:

> ~~Dear G,~~

> ~~We didn't have to end this way~~

and the second:

> ~~My dearest G,~~

> ~~Will you ever forgive me~~

then the third:

> Love,

> You should have seen it coming.

—it will tell a different story than if I placed
a length of twine beside a bracelet's clasp
and, beside those, a piece of shattered tumbler
from the bar where he might have wrapped
his thick fingers around her wrist and

dragged her into the icy air and where she
staggered onto the sidewalk and spat
in his face before heaving her guts.

It might say all that or it might show
how the desiccated perennial gestures
towards the purple beneath her eyes and
the crumpled tin mimics the gut's folds
when she's coiled into herself, and those
crossings-out transcribe all we mean
and don't—brittle petal, bent charm, frayed
cord, and a placard on the wall that reads:

I Burned Us In Ritual
2011
Chlorophyll, Sulphur, Brass, Blood, and Salt

HERE IS NO BIG LOVE FOR YOUR
BIG HEART, LITTLE ONE

I asked the woman what her necklace was made of.
It looks like shell, I said, *or flat, jagged stone*
She told me it was made of my skull

and that she had peeled
each piece from the wall
and floor

and washed the red away
and polished the shards
until they gleamed.

They look beautiful against your skin, I said.
Striking, truly.

DEHELIXING ADORA: A DEEP STRUCTURE PURGE

Phonetically, it's atavulga lorgenglock.
Alphabetically, ellemenophilia.
I have been liaisolusional, knelt at mirage.
My tongue raw from lapping at sand.
Nostalgillogical, I've fondled this rotten
sack of skeevish signifiers a trifle too long.
Any sense made's a shame. A little
righteous rage whets beauty the good sort
of crooked for flaying. Filet this given.
Debone the pronoun. I learn what it takes
to extricate: my language loosening its embrace
of *you*. So, *adieu . . . adieu . . .* fly free, flea-bat!
Fly! Fly, and elsewhere plague.

THE LONG CON

Of a tongue half stump, half parasite
and its slick mimicry is how I crowd

a room with fictions, tuft and pad
the mangle I sleep in with soft trash:

hair, plastic, fishing line. Wet click
of window latch holding open a mouthful

of rough breeze that whittles leaves
into shivs of light. I sew wolves in

wool, stitch teeth into burlap, a slip
to shield one from the sun's idiot joy,

which forgets for the minute it needs to;
that green, too, will rust. Because

what wild red fruit I'll pinch into
my palm's shallow bowl swims

into mind the freak tenderness of his
hand tucking a stray curl behind my ear

before it struck, an imprint of shimmer
as blood pricks up through skin

the way light, when a harder wind
gusts, shimmers through leaves, the same

light we believe draws us close, reckoning
burn to blush our shoulders. Because heat

conjures gratitude now that we
anticipate ice shelves shearing free

plagues striated in glacier and sediment
and shouldn't the end thus sweeten
any grunt escaping their mouth and mine?

When Skies Are Grey

Between's the murk.
What warmth we scavenge:
perishable as any body.

Know a fuck's
elision, not liaison.

Not: *mon‿ami*   *mon‿amour*
But: *l'homme*   *aujourd'hui*
Do not mistake me.

Day's only tilt
and spin abstracted.
What the sun does

we will call morning.
What it doesn't, night.

1:11

one liest, to
weave her meal
three says:

no body saw
and we won't
tell. cochineal

crushed shell
red, diest.

widow. riddle.
the luck
of one tangled
in her silks.

it does
take two.

the starved.

the food.

BEGINNING

♥

poetry is senseless / like some violence

Love Song

I want to make
everything sound

unbearably plain.
Meanwhile, the world is

always my shame returned.
That is, nothing you can say

will tear me away from

la la la la la la la la la la

means

THE LEAST I CAN DO

he hands me
the bricks

with which i build
a very tall wall

. . .

a very tall wall
which i build with

the bricks
he hands me

VOICE / VICE

Always, an other—stirs, stirring
calls you away. Dove's coo.
A neighbour's unimpeachable
whistle, its pitch arrowed through O's
of smoke he chuffs out the drawn
purse of a mouth. Have your shadows
been accounted for
          —said the limelight to the player
          in no stage called the world.

You can tell I'm the devil
by all these sibilants, by my crossed
seas, and how I spell every objective
correlative into snakes. The car door shut
quits their laughing. Open, an occasional
cackle rises from the joy drone. Here
is that dance I do so well
          to the one song you know
          all the words to
                    sing sing   sing sing sing

SLANT

crooked / fucked

◆

deceive / relive

◆

relief / bereaved

◆

felt / left

◆

adored / read

◆

hard / heart

◆

cold / reeled

◆

liar / sure

◆

promise / facile

◆

love / leave

I : Her : She

i project
my-

self astrally
beg a book o-

pen, come smear
oily finger-

prints on my parch-
ment, an ache

poetics. agog
at her own

argot's promise shaded
in indigonian Sans-

krit. fronds cool
forehead shining

milky chrism poured
over her, chosen.

NOT A MERMAID

those aren't gills
someone has

cut slits
into your neck

Someone No One Everyone Anyone

and I put all this blood in, but things just get sticky
No one's a mess anyone

wants to pick up after, so I marched my ass down
to the shack that flashed

LIVE MODELS in red and asked if they needed
someone good with light.

Everyone was bronzed
and someone was covered in glitter.

"Here," I said, "hold
that glow

lower" and motioned to someone
who shone a weird green

light so high
the shadows made everyone's eyes onstage look

like pulsing suckholes.
Limbs in that angle

seem tentacled with darknesses.
I tsked, "That's no way to shine a body."

Lucy / The Halo-Halo Remix

Fathoming outside the blob: gotta get over
that hump. List virtuosities, my ecstatic
hystorics. Unbuckle this bliss. You go
daddydaddy a hailstorm in three-inchers, I will
flatline the lolling-tongue pup herd, serial
and milk aisle. Come skim my cream, kitty,
and lick it like you mean it. Dog days
of chlorinated, rolling nine deep, crashing
complexes to swim in, not an ocean
for yards or years. My simulacrum so good
he's for realing, heavy breathing on speaker
fondest and fondling. Maybe left on
a curb: foundling. He was center of skewed
valences, I am circumference, but dive-
bombed radial, spoke like sun rays (8)
yellow yolk flanked in red (war), blue
(peace)—Poet, please! Ang tula ko's
a shade between caramel and calyx
pistil-blasted, I'm damndest, turning over
souls, selling 'em back to baba Bael,
telling him: My Goodness Is Alchemical.
My Every Lineament, A Faultless Gold.

Like, Literately

May I be embraced? My mode
nasciturs, does not converse.

Once, to a folderol, I antiquated the dowel rod
for purposes of wand and gait (y' know ...

trick and pilgrimage).

Some call mine a bothersome affliction
but I mumble, *penumbra's the fun of it.*

Here, eat the locals.
I have broken and buttered their soft hot centers.

Why doubt my hospitality?
I am inviting you into my sentence.

Four roses and seven thorns, a crow
battered its sleek head against

the point.

MIDDLE

All This Paper

And no more evenings
to fold into cranes.

Let us light the path
of gasoline snaking

towards the tinderbox
of his Buick. I was too

young to remember.
The back seat, the basement, the stall.

Membranous, maybe.
Or friable. Sheaves

peeled. Many misplaced
contexts ago. Give me mine

back. I go on
predicating as if

conditional. Led
to feed, or what teeth

clamped shut on my ankle
so long I learned to love

licking the raw seam.
Who's fool enough

to step into the same river
twice drowns in her paradox

recovering for all
who survive her

a little peace
bloating at the hook.

LATE OCTOBER

Don't say lost.
North is nowhere and you
are not home. Eat these

crisp red leaves. Like the child
we saw, fistfuls of brittle fire,
mouth loud with crackling.

Or another who broke
out of his mother's hold, again
and again, gaze fixed

into the middle distance
where nothing takes shape.
In this place

trees bleed before
they're bare. Fall's gold
hits me in the chest.

I think, what the fuck
did we do to deserve this?
It is so beautiful I feel obscene.

One after the Other

Luminous with lack I billow invertebrate
in salt and algal dark. A thing making sense
one human at a time in this lean doom.

The narrative, inviolate, declines
chromatically. I order my days by depth
of hue. Light is sensible and fathoms

where history refused. Before self
shades into name, the foreground spores
atomic. Swaths of nothing to call

back, or by her name. Loitered at doors
coming or going, was I set against
four walls or the shore and sand?

Does the story confuse its tense?
Does she cohere like skin, how it holds
our hells together, syntax and sheath.

If you believe, there may still be hope.
I might still convince you when someone
happens in my life the minutes undulate

and bloom. And anthers of stamen
burst to cloud my flight, void
of story, all flaw and collapse.

Let me suspend your dread for awe.
Let me care for you in our time of lead.
Reels re-imagine her unbroken

and nameless until I name her, unmade.
Before maker, she makes herself a thing
making sense in this lean doom, regardless

of what in fact happened, is happening—
the ground or occan to swell her heavy
sunk in a salt and algal dark, all light, all lack.

MANTRA

Because I never figured it would be this easy.
And ruin's not so slow as they'd have you believe.
Beyond the privacy of the mistakes we choose
live others, mistaken, in small quiet rooms.
I smell boot polish. Head, asphalt.
Before a press of tread at the temple, a bolt
splits my sight. I taste iron, salt.
Only the rain beats softly on my window.
Here's warm. Kind guides insist there are so
many feelings to attend to. I spoke to who
asked what my pyrotechnics dazzle to conceal.
All I can hold, I assured. Nothing I feel
is fit to say plain. We are composed of ordinary
sorrows. If I thumb beads to splinter, the worry
only gives me away. Mind's not worth the dime
it turns on. And soul? Less. Take the last time
I pleaded, *Father, forgive me.* But quiet does
enough. Certainly no less, and these days
enough's all we're good for. The rest is just
letting on, which I will not live. I commit
or am committed to. What convicts, and all I am
convicted by. I swallow words, or flesh, or crumbs.

IN PRAISE OF WHAT CONTAINS

Of course I make it about the body.
What else will measure? A night,

alone, I stroke the keloid scar
pearled on my knee. I keep

putting things in my mouth
to figure out what they mean.

In bed she says, one day it won't be
so spectacular. But it isn't about

what's seen or even touched.
This let you in. Think of all it takes.

Autopoiesis

Nothing will permit me to return.
All real processes are irreversible.
Ash is only that which can't unburn.

Nor will what slithers to be born
take wing. The incontrovertible
nothing forecloses my return.

Our singing suggests we yearn
for the scale, the stave, the table.
All left in song is all we cannot burn.

And all in verse is nothing we can learn.
And though they say *as soon as you are able*—
nothing will permit me to return.

Not home, nor him, nor the letter torn
then taped together, can hold or reassemble.
Ash is only that which can't unburn.

Not ghosts, only so much smoke to warn
of fires ahead. And after, the inassimilable
dark erases any path; what's edgeless nulls return.

This second law allows us to discern
the *complex and natural* from any invariable
nothing—to and from which I must return.
Ash is only that which can't unburn

On The Topography of Tears

1.

An article I read on the molecular composition of tears claimed tears of grief look different than, say, tears of anger, or of slicing onions, or of joy. It featured a photographer who for eight years collected her tears, and the tears of people she knew, shed in moments of various heightened feeling. She set these tears on slides and captured their image using an optical microscope. The article seemed to suggest that enzymes and minerals arrange themselves emotionally. It is an interpretation or a hoax or the fiction of anything composing itself. What you make, and make up, and make up for.

The photographer, who must also be a poet, describes the loops and patterns in these micrographs as "places, landscapes", and likens the entire series to "an ephemeral atlas". She writes, "tears are the medium of our most primal language".

The pictures are pretty, but the idea swells only to quickly deflate. Even if one sort of crying is more or less chemically bitter or sweet, even if bliss splinters into crystals and loss warps like punctured honeycomb, under glass, it's all the same: your face contorts into someone you'll swear isn't you. No matter the salts charting your skin, no map of the interior resolves into view. It isn't and will never be you, blotchy and puffy, crumpled inward, making a noise that's nothing like language.

2.

to believe coming home sutures the ground split under your feet—is
nostalgia

to believe broken's made whole in the telling; that is, to begin, middle,
and end it so; that is, to return again and again, changing a word, a
break, a full stop—is sentimental

to believe recovering a language amounts to more than what a tongue
gets used to—is nostalgia

to say *I love you* and believe it is the same *I*, the same *love*, the same
you—is sentimental

to believe you can cross oceans and mountain ranges without the
horizon's blade slicing you neat in two—is nostalgia

to believe everything you cannot bring back still breathes, is breathing
now, that you breathe even now—is sentimental

to believe in the business end of a pen—is nostalgia

to believe nothing ends—is sentimental

3.

tears
configure
landscape

does nothing
like language
get through

is it true
when you cried
what you meant

Nostos, a Longing

I learned the myth of a mother
rejecting her animal infant by scent

but remain half-convinced
of the touch that mars a child

estranged, the way a thumb
measuring an in-between

distance just as soon might
smear my name illegible, a black

streak, the negative of meteor
debris tracking a wish across

white sky. No less the wake
of a folded boat along

a canal, paper buffeted past
bottle throats, snags of glass, all

discarded, iridesced. And, in our
wishing, we scavenge what glitters

in the dreck. Because any exile
believes herself a changeling, taken in.

And all her beloveds, duped.
A doubling like common time, or

how a slow shutter resolves into
an exposure of ghost—in silver

nitrate, gelatin. Or, if written,
the trope replaces waking up, when,

dispersed by morning, we ask no one
who'll answer—*where am I? Where am I now?*

Go-To

When it's been told, all told, every lifetime
I revisit, stroke of nostalgia atomizing
clementine, or chlorine, some scent
I recognize, or don't, but fold into
new convolutions, the same story re-
ordering my days and verbs ahead, and I
can't for the line of me extract any more
than: I am
tired. I am tired
of myself when I think
of you and nowhere we are
headed towards, the last word
always
the first, again. Again.

Acknowledgements

The following journals have published work in this manuscript:

The Awl: "Someone No One Everyone Anyone"
Bat City Review: "Lucy," "Lucy, Again," and "Lucy / The Halo-Halo Remix"
Bennington Review: "Go-To"
DIAGRAM: "Leave the Sky to Who Shall Wear"
DREGINALD: "Sentimental Poem," "Narrative Poem," "Stop Me If You've Heard," "Spell," "When Skies Are Grey"
Cream City Review: "My Demon Is Sad All It Can Be Is Complicit"
Fields: "Dehelixing Adora: A Colonial Kantá (published as "A Colonial Madrigal"), "Dehelixing Adora: A Deep Structure Purge," "Dehelixing Adora: At the Tip of His Tongue"
Hardly Doughnuts: "Behind the Shelf" (published as "She Describes for Him Very Slowly"), "here is no big love for your big heart little one"
Hayden's Ferry Review: "On *The Topography of Tears*"
Nat. Brut: "Slant," "1:11"
Parcel: "Mantra"
Seneca Review: "Scene Rewrite"
The Journal: "Making New Friends"
Yalobusha Review: "Halfway," "Nostos, A Longing"

Thank you, Kelley Roberts and Raymond McDaniel, for guiding me to truth and for teaching me to be brave. Thank you, Lacey Drummond, for your shining kindness. Thanks, francine j. harris, for showing me how it's done. Thank you, Brooke Axtell, for your fierce spirit. Thank you, Zoe Tuck, for your tender brilliance. Thanks to Jill Essbaum Peng, Jessica Piazza, Paisley Rekdal, and to all the incredible writers and teachers I've been so fortunate to work with and learn from. And thank you, Max Seawright, for your heart and for painting me the stars.

About the Author

Paula Mendoza earned her BA in English at the University of Texas and her MFA in Poetry at the University of Michigan, and is currently pursuing a PhD in Creative Writing at the University of Utah. Hyphenated, she's Filipino-Canadian. Regionally, an Austinite. Mostly, her home's in words. She lives and writes in Salt Lake City, Utah.

About Gaudy Boy

From the Latin *gaudium*, meaning "joy," Gaudy Boy publishes books that delight readers with the various powers of art. The name is taken from the poem "Gaudy Turnout," by Singaporean author Arthur Yap, about his time abroad in Leeds, the United Kingdom. Similarly inspired by such diasporic wanderings and migrations, Gaudy Boy brings literary works by authors of Asian heritage to the attention of an American audience. Established in 2018 as the imprint of the New York City–based literary nonprofit Singapore Unbound, we publish poetry, fiction, and literary nonfiction. Visit our website at www.singaporeunbound.org/gaudyboy.

Winners of the Gaudy Boy Poetry Book Prize
Autobiography of Horse, by Jenifer Sang Eun Park
The Experiment of the Tropics, by Lawrence Lacambra Ypil

Fiction
The Foley Artist, by Ricco Villanueva Siasoco
Malay Sketches, by Alfian Sa'at